Mandy, Mindy, Misty
by
Shelly York

Dedication

This story is dedicated to all "our girls," our shelties Wimsey and Kenzie, their ancestor Melody, and their distant descendant Lacy, along with their best friends, yorkies Heather and her distant descendant Lily. The story is wholly fictional, but the ideas for it grew out of the wonderful interactions of Wimsey, Kenzie, and Heather.

Acknowledgments

The author and his wife, Carolyn, have been blessed by a succession of wonderful shelties, Melody, Wimsey, Kenzie, and Lacy. The girls' best friends, Heather and Lily, have been the delight of our friends Virginia and Jack Lee, and all references to Heather and Lily are made with their kind permission.

Cast

Mandy .... Wimsey
Mindy .... Heather
Misty .... Kenzie

Stand-ins and Stunt Doubles

Melody for Wimsey as Mandy.
Lily for Heather as Mindy.
Ronald Gordon Munro for Shelly York as author.

Production Logo

Lacy as Lacy.

Illustrator

All the illustrations in this book were the artistic creations of
Ronald Gordon Munro.

Mandy, Mindy, Misty
by Shelly York

1: Mandy

Mandy lay upon her pillow,
  still asleep upon her bed,
Resting warm and very comfy
  in her coat of russet red.
Her chin was gently resting
  on her paws of gleaming white,
While her eyes were closed in slumber
  as she dreamt away the night.

From the window came the dawning
  of the rising, shining sun,
Bringing promise of the glory
  of a day just now begun.
By the gleaming, shining, glinting
  of its streaming, beaming light,
Came the sun in rays of wonder
  now to play in Mandy's sight.

In a dance of flashing dazzle
    did the sun begin its game,
From the top of Mandy's forehead,
    down her nose and up the same.
"Way too early, way too early"
    thought Miss Mandy of this dance
As her eyes were coaxed and prodded
    wide enough to take a glance.

From a nest beyond the window,
    on a branch upon a tree,
Came the twirling, chirping sing-song
    of some song birds singing free.
Those song birds from the meadow
    who could fly upon the wing,
Came a-chirping and a-chanting
    with the song they loved to sing.

Feed me now.
Feed me now.
I want a worm today.
I want a worm today.
Feed me now.

"Way too early, way too early"
  thought Miss Mandy of this song,
"Let me nap a little longer,
  til another comes along,
Like the ringing and the dinging
  of the ticking-tocking clock,
Or the swirling, swooshing, swishing,
  of the steaming shower spout."

Clinking-clanging was the answer
  in response to Mandy's wish,
From the far and distant kitchen
  where a spoon now clinked a dish.

Ears alert!
Head up high!
Nose to sniff what's drifting by!

Deep and rich upon the nose
  is a smell the tummy knows.
Soft and sweet to fill a sigh
  is the fragrance of a pie.

Such is wisdom in the making
   of a puppy's dawning day,
Just enough to cause a sheltie
   to be up and on her way
To a kitchen filled with clinking
   in a cozy breakfast nook,
To a kitchen's fragrant feasting
   where awaits the breakfast cook.

2: Mindy

In a house not far away,
Oh, it isn't far at all,
In a house with many bushes
And with trees, straight and tall,

Lives a friend who greets each morning
With a song she oft recites
Just to thank the sun for bringing us
Its rays of shining light.

"Here's to the morning,"
She barks with eager ease,
"Here's to the daylight,
May it shine for all to please."

This cheerful, charming puppy,
Who greets each day the same,
Answers bright and quick to "Mindy"
If you call her by her name.

A yorkie small of stature,
But, oh, so very big of heart,
She rises sharp each morning
Just to praise its faithful start.

Quick she dashes to the window
To look across the lawn,
To catch the fleeting flashes
At the first light of dawn,

To watch the gleaming sunlight
As it passes through the trees
Where it spreads its rising beauty
Over all the shimmering leaves.

Oh, to be a puppy!
To romp and chase and run,
To play in all that glory
Given freely by the sun.

Mindy prances to the music
That the morning sun begins,
Then she dances to the rhythms
That fly upon the wind,

She whirls with excitement
When her name is said out loud,
For she knows she'll soon be playing
Out beneath the puffy clouds.

Over there, along the bushes,
Is where Mandy likes to play,
Very near the place where squirrels live,
Who tease her every day.

Mandy romps among the bushes,
Mindy scurries round the tree,
And everywhere the one is found,
The other, too, is sure to be.

3. Clanging! Banging!

Behind the yard where Mandy plays
And Mindy romps 'most every day,
Where no one thinks to be surprised,
Stands a fence of goodly size.

Through the panels of the fencing,
If you happen to be glancing,
In a glimpse you might be casting
Just to see what might be passing,

In the winking of your eye,
It just happens you might spy,
In an odd, peculiar scene,
A charming yard, rather bright and green.

And this yard of flowers, trees, and more,
Where birds come flocking by the score,
Is oddly quiet and serene,
Where no one's ever, ever seen!

But, on this day, this very day,
Having chased and raced at play,
Nestled now on grassy patches
'Neath a tree's broad leafy branches,

As their heads were nearly nodding,
Nearly napping, gently rocking,
Suddenly, there came a clanging,
As if someone sharply banging,
Banging hard upon a door.

"What's that racket? What's that racket?",
  barked Miss Mandy in a shout,
"On your paws now, twist and turn,
  til we know what's come about!"

"To the fences! Whirl and bark!"
Called Miss Mindy quick and sharp,
"Let's go see what's all the matter
In this rowdy clang and clatter!"

So then barking, twisting, whirling,
Off they ran in gallant dashes,
Down the fence and round the corner,
Turning back like streaking flashes.

Oh! The wonders that they saw
Through the cracks they looked between,
Right before their very eyes:
Strangers! Never known, never seen!

And the boxes that they carried,
Up the stairs and through the door,
Could it mean these frightful strangers
Would be neighbors evermore?

Hours past and still they came,
Boxes big and boxes small,
Chairs and beds and tablecloths
Piled up high against a wall.

When at last the clamor ended
And no clanging filled the air,
Once again the yard was silent,
Like no noise was ever there.

"What a puzzle," barked Miss Mandy.
As she sniffed the air once more,
"What became of all the people
And the clanging of the door?"

"What became of all the ruckus?"
Barked Miss Mindy in reply,
"It's as though it never happened."
"How very strange to not know why."

But, for puppies who would ponder,
Reasons why would have to wait,
For this day was quickly passing,
And the hour had grown late.

4. Misty

On the morrow that did follow,
When the sun was shining bright,
Mandy thought the yard was quiet;
Mindy thought it seemed all right.

"Yet, it happened as we saw it,"
Thought Miss Mindy of that day,
"All that noise and all that clanging,
Surely came, then went away."

Mandy, too, was surely puzzled
As she strolled along the fence,
Sniffing out some simple reason
That at last would make some sense.

As they happened to be glancing
Through the fencing they were passing,
Of a sudden to their eyes
Came a sight of some surprise.

"Oh my goodness," started Mindy,
"Oh good gracious, can it be?"
"It's a sheltie," finished Mandy,
"Underneath the neighbor's tree!"

Leaning hard against the fencing,
Mindy gained a better view,
Then she jumped to bark a warning,
"Why, she looks a bit like you!"

And, indeed, among the bushes
And beneath the neighbor's tree,
Hither, thither in a dither
Came a puppy roaming free.

She was searching in the bushes.
She was sniffing with her nose.
She was poking under branches
And then scratching with her toes.

Mindy frowned her brow with worry,
And she did a double whirl,
But Miss Mandy was uncertain;
Should she bark or merely twirl?

Miss Mindy was the older
And more worldly of the two,
So the chore of speaking boldly
Came to her, as was her due.

"On your guard against this stranger,"
Said Miss Mindy very wise,
"Remember all the strangeness
Right before our very eyes!"

"First a noise came sharply banging,
Then the air was filled with clanging.
Now this stranger here appears
Where all that noise had filled our ears!"

"We must be wary of intrusion
When it comes from such confusion.
She's a sheltie, yes, that's true,
But she's really not like you!"

"She is smaller in her stature,
And her fur is darker brown,
And her ears are rather floppy,
Always tipped and hanging down."

"Her tail is bent and crooked
And her teeth aren't even straight.
She'll win no prize from judges;
They'll just stick her in a crate."

"So, I think I'm going to bark at her
And make this very clear,
She's no friend to be around us,
And she's not to venture near."

So Miss Mindy gave a warning
In a yap both sharp and clear,
"You're no friend; you're just a stranger.
Don't you dare come over here!"

Turning then to nudge Miss Mandy,
Mindy quickly bound away.
"Let's show this nervy stranger
Just how friends are meant to play!"

Off they trotted through the bushes
In their favorite game of chase,
But Miss Mandy's eyes kept searching
For the stranger's longing face.

"She's a sheltie," thought Miss Mandy,
"And of that I should be glad.
So, why am I unhappy,
And she with eyes so sad?"

5. No Stranger Than a Friend

What a quandary! What a worry!
  Poor Miss Mandy was upset!
What to do about a stranger
  when you haven't even met!

Mindy too began to rue
  the stranger's sorry end.
Was it mean not to play with her?
  Could not a stranger be a friend?

But, no time to worry, not today,
  whether friends could be or not.
There were things to do and games to play
  before it got too hot.

So, to the bushes trotted Mandy
  where a squirrel might soon be found,
But all was quiet there this morning,
  not one squirrel was on the ground.

And all was quiet, too, beneath the tree
  where Mindy's toys now lay,
For they didn't seem to be as fun
  as they were just yesterday.

"Oh me, oh my," Miss Mandy sighed,
  "why do we feel so sad?
With all these many things to do,
  we should really feel quite glad."

Then they both lay down beneath a tree
   where the shade was cool and dark,
And on their paws they placed their chins,
   way too weary now to bark.

As their eyes were dimly dozing
   and their lids were firmly closing,
In the silence came a rumbling
   like a giant tummy grumbling,
Grumbling overhead and falling down.

 Stand alert!
   Paws foursquare!
What's that rumbling
   in the air?

In a stance that stood no nonsense,
   Mandy turned to quickly glance
Up the trees and down the bushes
   and all along the fence.

Mindy too sprang to her paws,
  then twirled right off the ground,
For overhead she saw the clouds
  that made those threatening sounds.

Dark they were,
  thick, and full of gloom,
Blotting out the sun
  like harbingers of doom.

Then suddenly there came a wind,
  and rain began to fall.
Lightning flashed across the sky,
  while booming thunder shook their paws.

Mandy howled against the wind.
  Mindy barked against the rain.
But nowhere could they find a place
  to save them from the storm that came.

Louder grew the wind
  until it seemed to roar.
It tore against the fence's gate,
  and cast it open like a door.

Mandy closed her eyes up tight,
  not to see the lightning flash,
While Mindy tried to hide her head,
  not to hear the thunder crash.

Suddenly, when all was lost,
  there came a streaking form
Who raced straight through the wind and rain
  and defied the very storm.

"Follow me!" the stranger barked,
    for, indeed, it was she who came.
"Follow me! I know a place
    where all is safe from wind and rain."

Mindy clung to Mandy
    who by the stranger now was led,
Across their yard and through the gate,
    into a dry and open shed.

"Saved!" barked Mindy
    "Saved!" and "Saved!" again,
While Mandy woofed and cheered
    just as happy as her friend.

Outside the storm was raging,
   but in the shelter all was dry.
Outside the flashing lightning blazed,
   but scarce a glimmer caught their eyes.

In the safety of the shelter,
   as they looked across the yard,
The thunder, too, seemed not so loud,
   and the rain seemed not so hard.

"You saved us," barked Miss Mindy,
   "We were lost, except for you.
How kind you must truly be,
   for it was more than we were due."

Then she drooped her head down very low
   because she knew that she'd been wrong
To think this caring stranger
   could not rightly here belong.

"We were mean when you came to play,
   and of this we are ashamed,
For you risked yourself to save us,
   and we don't even know your name."

"My name's Misty," woofed the stranger
    in a tone quite soft and shy,
"I only did as I was taught:
    to do what's right, or at least to try."

"But we were very much unkind,"
    barked Mandy still upset,
"You didn't owe us anything.
    You could have left us cold and wet."

"Kindness," Misty gently woofed,
  "isn't given as a trade.
It's freely offered, all of it,
  to all in need of help or aid."

"But, if ever I would have you be,
  even once, just kind to me,
Then surely I should be to you
  kind and generous too."

Then, in a bright and sparkling bark,
  Mindy whirled around and cheered,
While Mandy danced a little prance
  with her eyes now bright and clear,

And together in a circle,
  right around where Misty stood,
They turned and danced a greeting
  that only puppies understood.

Of a sudden, then, they stopped.
  Misty twirled upon her spot.
Then all three against the ground
  braced their paws and turned around.

Then the rousing, cheering, howling,
  that these puppies all were sounding
Soon gave way to leaps and boundings
  and the glee of tousled tumblings,
Tumblings of a joyful kind.

Oh, what a sight to see,
  this tumbling, jumbling jamboree.
No better friends could ever be,
  who had such spirits set so free.

What great wonders
  words can open
When in friendship's cause
  they're spoken.

As kindness may enrich our lives
  with selfless acts and deeds,
Friendship may our spirits bless
  in ways that soothe our darkest needs.

Outside the storm was easing,
  and the rain was quickly leaving,
And as the clouds that filled the sky
  were growing light and passing by,

The air grew brisk and crispy,
  and the clouds grew thin and wispy,
And all within this shining scene
  seemed newly fresh and freshly clean.

Then, in a burst of furry frenzy,
  in a blaze of whirling twirling,
Came three puppies brashly dashing
  in a manner fast and flashing.

Mandy pranced and Mindy danced,
  while Misty romped clear once around,
And in a chorus of good cheering,
  they did woof a joyful sound.

In such manner did they play
  until the very end of day.
Then each went home to dream that night
  a puppy's dream of true delight,

For in that dream, three puppies played,
  and all were best of friends.
They were Mandy, Mindy, Misty,
  friends, in all and every end.

** The End **

Made in the USA
Las Vegas, NV
28 April 2021